Contents

What to Do 2

A Disaster 4

A Bee Mystery 6

Why are Bees Disappearing? 8

What Some Scientists Think 10

Answers to the Mystery 12

More Ideas 14

Something to Think About 16

Do You Need to Find an Answer? 18

Do You Want to Find Out More? 19

Word Help 20

Location Help 23

Index 24

What to Do

Choose a face

Remember the colour you have chosen.

When you see your face on the page, you are the LEADER.

The LEADER reads the text in the speech bubbles.

There are extra words and questions to help you on the teacher's whiteboard. The LEADER reads these aloud.

When you see this stop sign, the LEADER reads it aloud.

STOP
My predictions were right/wrong because . . .

You might need:

- to look at the WORD HELP on pages 20–22;
- to look at the LOCATION HELP on page 23;
- an atlas.

If you are the **LEADER**, follow these steps:

1 PREDICT

Think about what is on the page.

- Say to your group:

"I am looking at this page and I think it is going to be about…"

- Tell your group:

"Read the page to yourselves."

2 CLARIFY

Talk about words and their meaning.

- Say to your group:

"Are there any words you don't know?"

"Is there anything else on the page you didn't understand?"

- Talk about the words and their meanings with your group.
- Read the whiteboard.

Let's check:

- Ask your group to find the LET'S CHECK word in the WORD HELP on pages 20–22. Ask them to read the meaning of the word aloud.

3 ASK QUESTIONS

Talk about how to find out more.

- Say to your group:

"Who has a question about what we have read?"

- Question starters are: how…, why…, when…, where…, what…, who…
- Read the question on the whiteboard and talk about it with your group.

4 SUMMARISE

Think about who and what the story was mainly about.

When you get to pages 16–17, you can talk to a partner or write and draw on your own.

 or

A Disaster

A tiny bee flying from flower to flower is very important to the world. For as long as people have lived, bees have helped to make the food that people eat. Bees **pollinate** the crops and help them grow.

Now, billions of bees all over the world are dying and no one really knows why. This is a **disaster** for the world. Many things would change without bees.

I am looking at this page and I think it is going to be about… because…

Are there any words you don't know?

Let's check: pollinate

Who has a question about what we have read?

What do you think might happen to the world if there were no bees?

A Bee Mystery

Thousands of bees have flown away from their hives and disappeared.

Bees can travel up to two miles looking for food, but they usually return to their hives. They can find their way back by following the special smell of their hive. They don't often get lost.

Some hives have been left full of honey and **larvae**. Bees don't usually leave honey for other bees to steal. They also don't usually leave their larvae to look after themselves.

I am looking at this page and I think it is going to be about... because...

Are there any words you don't know?

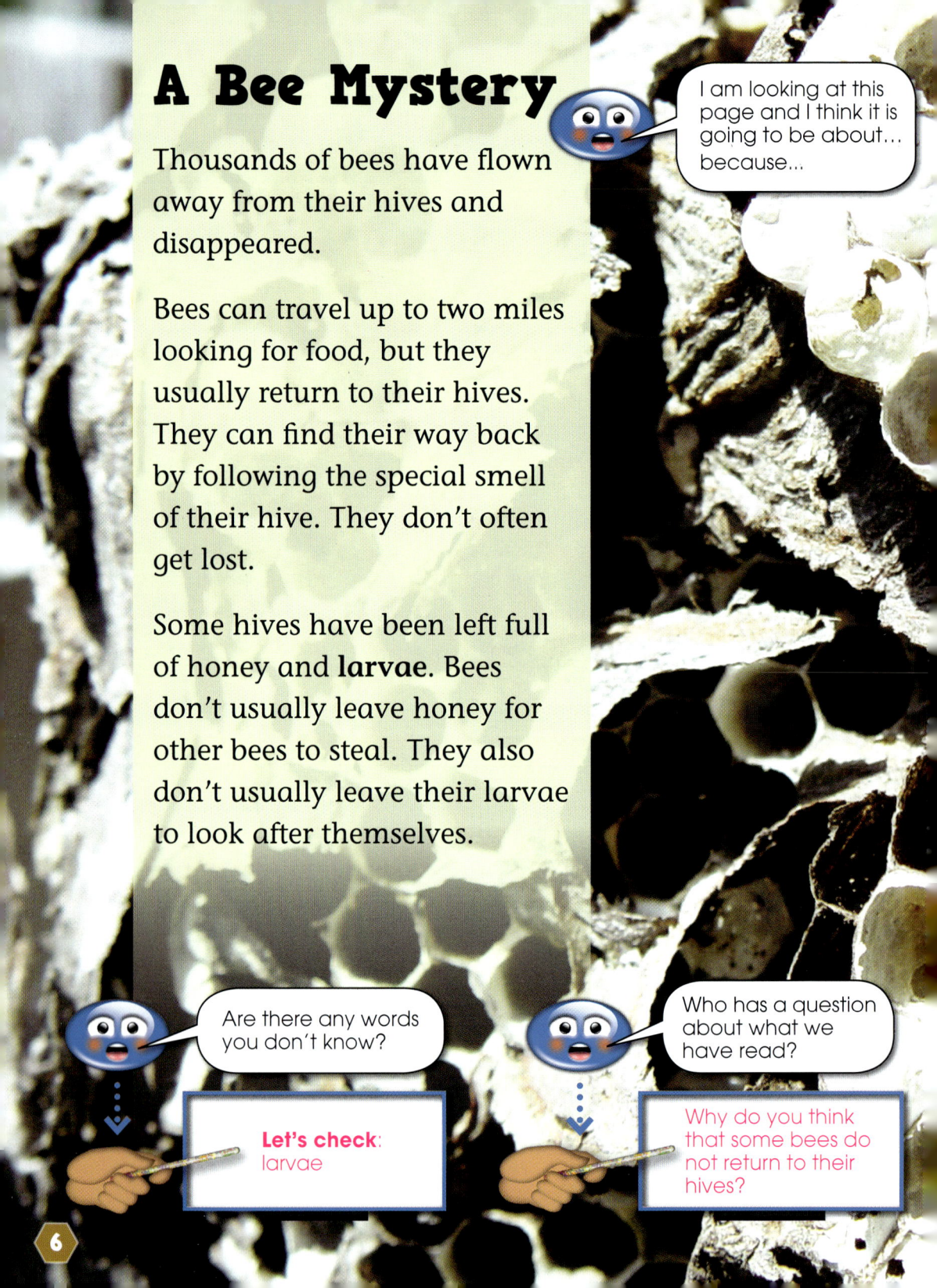

Let's check: larvae

Who has a question about what we have read?

Why do you think that some bees do not return to their hives?

Why are Bees Disappearing?

Scientists and beekeepers are trying to solve the mystery of the disappearing bees.

Some scientists have **examined** dead bees. They have found that the bees are not very healthy at all.

Scientists think that one reason bees are dying is because of **mites**. Mites are tiny insects that **cling** onto bees. The mites can make the bees sick and they die. Mites can destroy a whole beehive.

I am looking at this page and I think it is going to be about… because…

Are there any words you don't know?

Let's check: examined

Who has a question about what we have read?

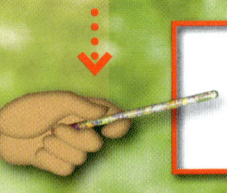

How do you think mites attach themselves to the bees?

What Some Scientists Think

I am looking at this page and I think it is going to be about... because...

Some scientists think that bees are disappearing because they have been **poisoned**. Farmers spray their crops to kill insects that are eating the plants. These sprays can make bees sick.

Bees also may not be getting enough food to stay strong. **Climate change** might mean the flowers open before the bees have woken from their winter sleep. Then the bees don't get the **nectar** and pollen that they need.

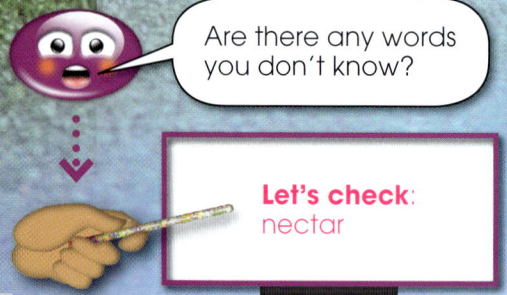
Are there any words you don't know?

Let's check: nectar

Who has a question about what we have read?

Why do you think bees may not be getting enough food?

Answers to the Mystery

I am looking at this page and I think it is going to be about… because…

It is very hard for scientists to find out why bees all over the world are dying. Most bees die away from their hives, so scientists don't have a dead body to look at for clues.

Some scientists are trying to find answers to the **mystery**. They have glued tiny **microchips** to the backs of bees. The microchips can send **signals** to the scientists. The signals let the scientists know where the bees are and where they have been.

Are there any words you don't know?

Let's check: microchips

Who has a question about what we have read?

How do you think it helps scientists to know where the bees are?

More Ideas

It is very important for scientists to learn all they can about how healthy bees are.

One scientist is testing bees to see if they return to the same **entry** holes in their hives. He has put shapes like triangles, rectangles and circles on the entry holes. Bees usually return to the same hole. If more bees go through a different hole, it might be a clue that something is wrong.

Everything must be done to help the bees in trouble.

I am looking at this page and I think it is going to be about… because…

Are there any words you don't know?

Let's check: entry

Who has a question about what we have read?

Why do you think some bees go through the wrong hole?

Bees can see colours and shapes. Most bees can tell the difference between a triangle and a circle.

This page was mainly about fact fact

STOP
My predictions were right/wrong because . . .

Something to Think About

 or

Clue

Think about what you have read about bees. What clues are there that bees are not well? Talk about your ideas with a partner, or write them down.

Do You Need to Find an Answer?

You could go to . . .

Library

Expert

Internet

Do You Want to Find Out More?

You could look in books or on the internet using these key words to help you:

honey bees

honey bee mystery

honey bee research

Word Help

Dictionary

climate change	change in the world's weather patterns that affects the behaviour of plants and animals
cling	hold on tightly
disaster	a sudden event that causes a lot of damage or loss of life
entry	a door or a place where something or someone can go in
examined	studied something closely
larvae	the early form of some animals
microchips	very small chips used to carry information
mites	tiny eight-legged animals related to spiders and ticks

mystery	something that is hard to understand or explain
nectar	a sweet liquid inside flowers
poisoned	harmed by a poison
pollinate	to pass pollen from one part of a plant to another to form seeds for new plants
signals	information sent by something like invisible radio waves

Word Help

Thesaurus

cling	grip, stick
disappeared	vanished
return	come back, come home
steal	raid, rob
travel	journey
trouble	problem
usually	often

Location Help

Bee Research Around the World

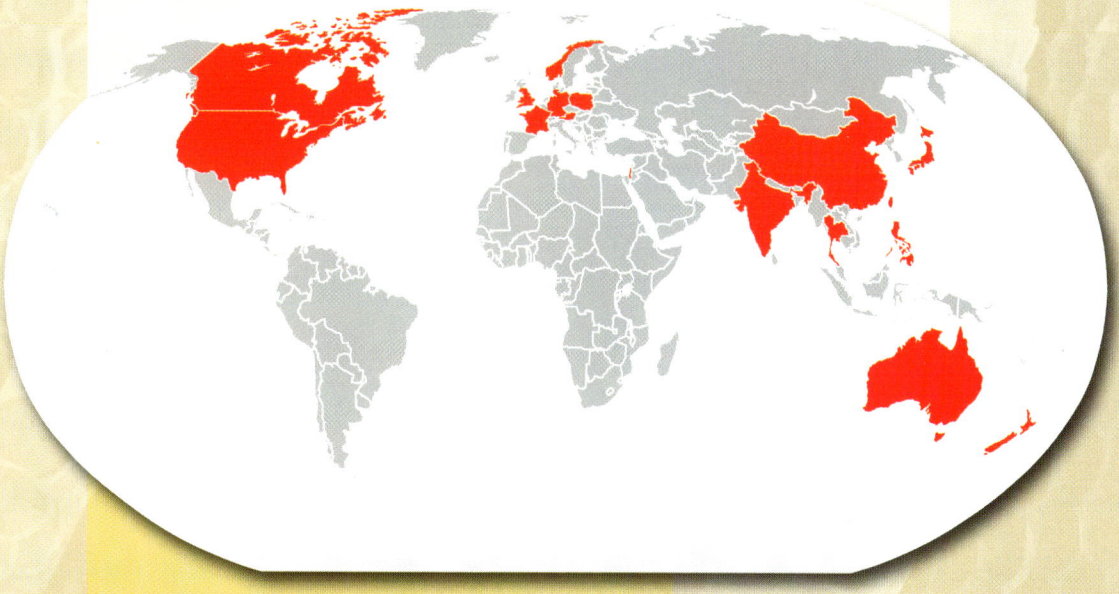

■ Countries where important bee research is taking place

Index

beekeepers 8

climate change 10

crops 4, 10

entry holes 14–15

flower... 4–5, 10

hive.. 6–7, 11, 14

larvae 6

microchips.. 12–13

mites 8–9

mobile phones 11

nectar 10

pollen 10

pollinate 4–5

scientists 8